Great Danes on a Plane

By Cameron Macintosh

Ted the Pug checked
the weight of the freight.

Then he put it on his plane.

"Eight dogs will ride
in the plane," said Lady
the Great Dane.

"Off we go, dogs!" Ted yelled.

Ted's plane went up and up!

Just then, Ted's tail
got a cramp.

Ted looked at Lady.

"I must have a break,"
he puffed.
"Can you fly the plane?"

"Yes, I can fly it!" said Lady.

"And I will help!" said Rex.

"Great!" said Ted.
"The dogs and the freight
must be safe!"

"Oh! I can not fit next to you,"
said Rex.
"It's too little for two Great Danes!"

"I will help from back here!"
said Rex.

"Great!" said Lady.

Rex got a map.

"That stick will make the plane go up!" said Rex.
"Then make the plane go left with your tail."

"Thanks, Rex!" said Lady.

Ted came back in.

"I think I am well," he said.
"I can land the plane."

"Did you fix your tail?"
said Lady.

"Yes," said Ted.
"My break was a big help."

Lady helped Ted land
the plane.

Rex helped with the map.

All the dogs and the freight
had a safe trip!

"Great job, Lady and Rex,"
said Ted.
"I will get you some steak!"

CHECKING FOR MEANING

1. How many dogs were on Ted's plane? *(Literal)*

2. Which two dogs helped fly the plane when Ted got a cramp? *(Literal)*

3. Why does Ted offer to buy Lady and Rex some steak? *(Inferential)*

EXTENDING VOCABULARY

freight	What is another word for *freight*? What types of freight are carried on a plane? Why would people put freight on a plane rather than on a train or truck?
cramp	What is a *cramp*? How does it feel? How can you make it go away?
steak	What is *steak*? What else do dogs like to eat?

MOVING BEYOND THE TEXT

1. How many pilots are there on a plane? Is it always the same number? Talk about what would happen if a pilot got sick during a flight.

2. What do pilots and the crew do to help keep people safe on a plane?

3. What are some reasons people fly from place to place on a plane rather than some other types of transport?

4. What can you see when you look out of the window in a large plane? Why?

SPELLINGS FOR THE LONG /a/ VOWEL SOUND

ay	ai	a_e	a	ea	eigh

PRACTICE WORDS

weight

freight

plane

Eight

Lady

Great

Dane

tail

break

safe

make

steak